YOUR
psychic
pathway
TO
JOY

ALSO BY SONIA CHOQUETTE

The Psychic Pathway

Your Heart's Desire

The Wise Child

True Balance

Your Psychic Pathway to New Beginnings

YOUR psychic pathway TO JOY

A SIMPLE GUIDE FOR LIVING LIGHTLY

Sonia Choquette, Ph.D.

Clarkson Potter/Publishers

NEW YORK

Published by Clarkson Potter/Publishers, New York, New York. Member of the
Crown Publishing Group, a division of Random House, Inc.
www.randomhouse.com

CLARKSON N. POTTER is a trademark and POTTER and colophon are registered
trademarks of Random House, Inc.

Material in this book was originally published in *The Psychic Pathway,*
Your Heart's Desire, and *True Balance.*

Printed in the United States of America

Design by Jane Treuhaft

Library of Congress Cataloging-in-Publication Data
Choquette, Sonia.
Your psychic pathway to joy : a simple guide for living lightly /
Sonia Choquette.—1st pbk. ed.
1. Parapsychology.   2. Spiritual life—Miscellanea.   1. Title.
BF1031 .C525   2002

133—dc21   2001054857

ISBN 0-609-61012-0

10 9 8 7 6 5 4 3 2 1

First Edition

We find our inner voice,
and the psychic pathway to joy,
in our hearts.

The heart leads the way to a broader, deeper understanding of both ourselves and others. It brings our attention to the subtle aspects of life and directs us toward a more creative, more loving, more healing approach to life's difficulties.

Intuition is the guiding voice of our hearts and a natural and important part of who we are. Without it we cannot find our way to our purpose and path in life. Without it we cannot truly discover what brings us authentic joy.

If you listen to your intuitive soul,

you walk with a gentle heart,

a joyous heart, the heart of a child.

joy

is a landmark of an intuitive life.

Living the intuitive life

is your greatest personal power.

Notice the subtle! It doesn't have to be a big deal to follow your intuition. In fact, it's rarely a big deal. Intuition is more often a series of unending "little deals" that make life easier and more joyful.

What favorite intuitive "little deals" have you experienced lately?

Be aware of the difference
between what is real and what is
actually a projection of your worries
and fears. Don't confuse your
greatest worries and darkest fears with
reality. If you do, you will eliminate all
possibility for the joy of the Universe
to grace your life.

four decisions
for inviting
MORE JOY
into your life

Be open to intuitive guidance every day.

Expect intuitive guidance on everything,
at every moment.

Trust your intuitive feelings.

Act on your intuitive feelings instead of
ignoring them.

The key to discovering what your heart desires is to pay keen attention to the world around you today. True intuition is the consequence of clear and accurate observations of the here and now. In your subconscious mind, such observations will lead to the most advanced and brilliant insights and help you create healing, balance, peace of mind, and a happy heart.

old rules

I don't know where I'm going.
I don't know what I'm doing.
I hope it works out.

new rules

I am happier when I trust
and use my intuition.
I don't need approval from others.
My success in life
will be my approval.

Slow down and enjoy the moment. You can't enjoy life if you are overbooked, juggling too many things at one time, or constantly playing catch-up and racing around like crazy. Being rushed reduces your awareness to a whirling gray fog of confusion. It also causes you to miss the subtle, intuitive, and healing guidance of your soul. So take a breath and relax! And it is not enough to intend to relax—actually schedule downtime into your appointment book.

MEDITATE

Meditation is the most effective way to
sharpen your awareness because it
clears away the mental noise and
distractions that prevent you from
noticing what is important
here and now. Meditation helps you
become more relaxed, balanced,
and present in the moment.
If you've never meditated, don't worry.
It's not difficult. It is quite simply
the art of relaxing your body,
resting your emotions,
and quieting your mind for
a few minutes a day.

Meditation is not another thing to do.

It is an invitation to stop doing.

Meditation begins with focusing on your breath. Start by taking in a deep breath right now and notice how much better you feel. Take a few more deep, cleansing breaths and then allow your breath to settle into an easy, rhythmic pattern. Next, gently close your eyes. Notice how relaxed you feel. With your eyes closed, continue to breathe in to the count of four, hold it to the count of four, and then exhale to the count of four. If thoughts arise, simply observe them and then go back to your breath. Don't fight or struggle with each new thought. Observe it as though it were one of a string of train cars moving through the night, entering into and then drifting out of your consciousness. Continue breathing and relaxing for fifteen minutes, then gently open your eyes and go about your day.

The best way to assure successful deep meditation is to be consistent. It is far more effective to meditate every day at the same time for fifteen minutes than to do so randomly once a week for an hour. I prefer to meditate in the morning upon waking and before getting out of bed. Perhaps this would be a good time for you as well. A busy schedule makes it tricky to find a consistent time to meditate, so you will have to select a time that works best for you. In the evening or after work may be ideal. Only you can know your schedule and its demands. Choose a time that is best suited for you and keep that appointment with your soul.

"I Am Calm"

This technique always works wonders
when you need a break.

Touch your thumb and forefinger together
on both hands, take a deep breath,
and say quietly to yourself
"I am . . ."
as you inhale and
". . . calm"
as you exhale.

Allow the feeling of calm to reverberate
throughout your entire body.

The act of touching thumb to forefinger
serves as a physical reminder to come back
to the moment, and the words
"I am calm" wash away the stress.

quieting

your nervous system
and nurturing yourself for a few minutes
can save you hours of wasted anxiety,
sudden blowups, hurtful confrontations,
health stress, and costly oversights.
It is a tonic for the spirit.

Clear the Drain

You can do this exercise whenever you feel you
need more time than you have.

Place both feet flat on the ground or floor and
let out a long, slow exhale.

Imagine that everything pressing down on you is
draining out of your body and into the ground
through the soles of your feet. Then, very slowly,
place your right hand over your heart and your
left hand over your belly. Take in a long,
luxurious breath while saying silently to yourself:
"I am present and relaxed."

Repeat the affirmation as you breathe out.

Do this exercise slowly five times
whenever you want to stretch time.
The key is to do it *very* slowly.

It takes four minutes at most, and it will
miraculously expand time.

Ten Ways to

LIFT YOUR SPIRIT

1. When you leave work, *leave work.*

2. Go for a walk with someone you love.

3. Invite friends over for a potluck dinner and board games.

4. Don't take phone calls during dinner.

5. Don't take work phone calls in the evening or on weekends.

6. Tell stories instead of watching TV.

7. Get a manicure or a pedicure.

8. Do something creative or artistic with your hands and give your mind a rest.

9. Write a long letter to a loved one.

10. Take a leisurely bubble bath while reading your favorite magazine.

Here's a good idea:
Sit down in front of an open window
and simply enjoy the view
for five minutes a day.

Ask
yourself:

Do I meditate regularly?

Am I practicing the thumb-forefinger stress buster?
(see page 19)

What was the best experience I had this week?

Is it difficult for me to be fully present? If so, what do I fear?

What are my three favorite ways to spend quality time
with my friends and loved ones? When was the
last time I did one of these three things?

Intuitive knowing is actually the art and the practice of listening with your heart, for it is there that the voice of inner wisdom speaks. It influences the way we take in information. Listening with the heart helps us focus on becoming aware of not only the *content* of information but its *intent*, its essence, as well.

Look for what is true,
what is real.
And trust what you discover.

TRUSTING
YOUR HEART

We all feel heart-based connections
from time to time because it is our
nature to do so. The problem arises
when we tune out or doubt
this inner sense of awareness,
surrendering instead
to the world of outside appearances
and opinions.

Two Ways to Listen to the Heart

Every time you need guidance, counsel,
direction, or simple reassurance from Divine
Spirit, close your eyes, take in a few deep,
cleansing breaths, and then place your
attention directly on your heart.

Allow your focus to rest there quietly
for a moment or two,
and then ask your heart to guide you.
Trust whatever feelings come up.
Don't censor or discount anything.
If nothing comes to you from the heart
immediately, don't worry.
Relax.

Remain open and patient.

Guidance will come before you know it.

A great way to open your heart is to actually place your hand over your heart and let it rest there as you speak and listen to another.

This gesture indicates that you are sharing your deepest truth and that you want to be truly heard.

It also conveys that you are truly willing to listen to another.
This is an especially effective technique for settling arguments and opening up troubled communication.

It clears away discord and allows real understanding and communication to occur.

One way to better hear your spirit
is to stop asking others
for their opinion.

SACRED SPACE

We are sensitive beings.
We are just as much in need of peace and
tranquillity as any other delicate creature.
We need to commit ourselves to creating such
a sacred environment for ourselves.
It's very hard to be joyful and open if we find
ourselves constantly subjected to confusing,
negative, and disruptive energy.
Insist on creating a calm and harmonious
environment in which to live.

Get rid of it! The first and most obvious way to create a peaceful home is to keep it clean and organized and filled with beautiful things that comfort your spirit. Everything is composed of energy, and everything you own absorbs your energy. The same holds true for negative energy. It, too, will linger in an atmosphere, oppressing you with its dreary and brittle vibration. If you live in messy, unloved, neglected disarray, you will come to resent it. The ugly environment itself discharges bad energy, and the resentment you feel because of it keeps recycling the negativity. The best cure for this problem is to clean and clear out or throw away all that isn't either necessary or soothing to your spirit. If an object is ugly, irritating, broken down, or useless, or if it reminds you of something or someone unpleasant, get rid of it! Given the effect it has on you, it isn't worth keeping.

Lighten up

While you are clearing out your home,
make sure that you simplify and purge your life
of all that is emotionally unnecessary as well.
Identify what is yanking on your attention
because of neglect and clean it up!
Take care of old business so that you can be
free to move on to new business.
Let go and complete the past so your soul
can lead you forward.

Create a Sacred Altar

A wonderful way to establish a healing vibration in your home is to create an altar. Set it up in a corner of your home where it will be left undisturbed, such as on a small table or box. It can even be set up on the floor if it won't be in the way. On your altar place objects, photographs, and talismans of the people and things you love. You can include religious icons and articles from nature—anything that lifts your spirit and moves you into your heart. You may also want to place fresh flowers, candles, or incense on your altar. Let your altar serve as a site for contemplation, reverie, meditation, and prayer. Eventually this sacred spot will become charged with the vibration of peace and serve as a healing place for you.

music

Listen to restful, meditative, or classical music to keep you clear, calm, and peaceful. The minute you listen to music, you leave your head and move into your heart. It's a known fact that Baroque music in particular, such as Bach, Vivaldi, Telemann, or Handel, calms the heartbeat and creates an inner state of tranquillity.

aromatherapy

Soothe your soul with aromatherapy. Aromatherapy fills the atmosphere with essential scents that are specifically known to calm, soothe, and uplift—oils such as lavender, chamomile, neroli, and rose. You simply put a drop or two of an essential oil on a lightbulb ring (available where essential oils are sold) in each room. The warmth of the lightbulb then diffuses the oil, filling the room with a subtle, beautiful aroma and energy. Taking a bath in these essential oils will soothe you just as well. Aromatherapy works directly on the nervous system, raising your vibration and bringing joyful energy directly to your spirit.

inhale!

Let the Universe support you.

You can fill your home with loving and positive vibrations by placing something living in each room: potted and flowering plants or pets, such as fish, birds, and turtles, as well as dogs and cats. Animals and plants fill a house with unconditional love and light. Both animals and plants have a very high, clear vibration. They will help you not only to clear out sadness, grief, anger, and depression but also to usher in the lighter, higher vibration of peace and joy.

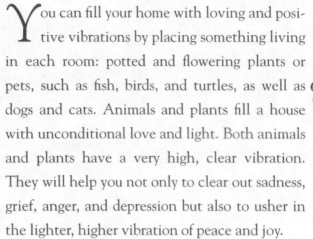

Bless Your House

First, light a candle,
and then walk from room to room,
asking Divine Spirit to bless your home.
As you bless the living room,
ask Divine Spirit to bring you pleasant
company and positive memories.
As you bless the kitchen, ask Divine Spirit
to nurture your body and soul.
As you bless the bedroom, ask Divine Spirit
to soothe and heal you as you sleep
and to bring you pleasant dreams.
Thank God in your own way
for providing you with safe haven and
sanctuary. Ask for continued protection
and blessings in your home.

You can also do this whenever you travel and
find yourself sleeping in another space.

Beautify
Your
Surroundings

The human spirit thrives on harmony, beauty, and balance. My spiritual teachers taught me that these qualities are essential to our soul's happiness; they are not optional. Bring this energy into your life. Paint your home in tranquil tones. Bring in fresh flowers. Place your furniture in pleasant arrangements. Eliminate clutter and disorder. Burn incense. Hang beautiful pictures and mirrors to enhance the light. Open the blinds and shades and let the light in. If your home is naturally dark, hang mirrors and burn full-spectrum lightbulbs to brighten it up. Light keeps energy moving. Love yourself enough to create harmony in every room.

peace and quiet

Loud and dissonant noises are disturbing to your spirit. So is music with negative lyrics, talk radio or television with hateful messages, malicious office or neighborhood gossip, as well as arguing, fighting, and cursing. To the best of your ability, keep the level and quality of sound around you, including the volume of televisions, stereos, and voices, positive and pleasant. Noise pollution and thought pollution steal your peace of mind. You must guard against these subtle saboteurs of your inner tranquillity. Be conscious of both how delicate you are and how your spirit needs a harmonious vibration.

The still, small voice of your heart
is the most direct personal affirmation
of God's love in your life.
Your experience will confirm that
this is true!

Ways to keep your energy clear
and your intuitive spirit joyful

Avoid emotionally charged situations.

Wait until you are calm and centered before
checking in with your intuition.

Don't expect your intuition to pass arbitrary tests.

Be curious, not controlling.

Explore without censoring yourself. If your intuition
is wrong, say "Oh well!" instead of "Oh no!"

Celebrate when your intuition serves you.

TRUST WHAT
YOU FEEL

Peace of mind and personal joy come from
paying as much attention to the
nonphysical dimensions of who you are as
you do to the physical dimensions.
This means acknowledging your vibes as
readily as you acknowledge red lights
and stop signs. It comes from noticing
whenever anything is off on any level
and choosing to listen to your intuition
so you can make changes that
will restore balance.
It's only when you trust your heart
and act on your instincts
that your spirit will remain on course
and moving in the right direction.

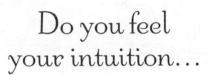

Do you feel
your intuition...

In your chest?

In your throat?

In your gut?

All over your skin?

Take a Mental Breather

One way to remain centered and lighthearted each day is to take mental breathers. Take one or two daily breaks of five to ten minutes to retreat from whatever you are doing and simply relax into a moment of tranquillity. These mental breaks can center on having a cup of herbal tea (not coffee—too much caffeine!), taking a quick stroll around the block, or simply sitting back and looking out the window. Taking mental breathers during the day will strengthen and tone your own vibration, rebalance any minor dissonance you may feel, and instantly lift your mood. Mental breaks create an inner oasis into which you can retreat whenever you are agitated, annoyed, or worried; they keep your own personal vibration clear and grounded and joyful.

When your spirit speaks to you
through your intuition, notice
how your body feels.
It feels solid, sound, honest.
It feels great!

Speak Up

Share your personal insights with
loving and supportive people. Sometimes
simply being able to share your intuitive
feelings with a sympathetic friend is
all you need in order to trust and act on what
your spirit is telling you. The right kind of
friend will help you honor your intuition.
Safely sharing your vibes with a soul supporter
will help you remain faithful to your heart.

One of the more exciting ways to tune in to your inner voice is to carry around a little pocket notebook or tape recorder. Every time you feel a hint, twinge, vibe, or subtle notion, simply write it down or record it. Do this instead of mulling it over and wondering whether or not it is valid, or ignoring it. Writing down or recording these feelings accomplishes several important things. First, it tells your subconscious mind that you now intend to notice and value your vibes. Second, it frees you from the temptation to ignore your intuition. Writing down or recording your perceptions clears your mind, and, if done regularly, it will provide you with feedback on what disturbs your joy and what ushers it in.

renewing connections

Remaining in touch with those you love is vital to your sense of personal joy and well-being. With so many people losing touch in today's fast-paced world, this becomes harder and harder to do. If you feel disconnected from people who are special to you, simply focus on your heart and think of them. Say their names to yourself and ask Divine Spirit to surround them with a pure white light of loving protection. Imagine this white light completely covering them wherever they are. See them in your mind's eye as safe, protected, and in total peace. Send them your love. And while you are at it, include yourself in this blessing as well. This simple exercise is almost always felt, and often the very person you envision will contact you soon after.

What If I'm Wrong?

When it comes to listening to intuition, being "right" shouldn't be your absolute goal, especially when you are just beginning to become more sensitive to energy. Accurately picking up on energy is a refined skill that develops with lots of practice and lots of errors if you are to become good at it. And besides, if you pick up troubling vibes, for example, and nothing seems to be amiss, don't be so sure you were off. You may be tuning in to a precarious moment, but the imbalance may correct itself somehow before it evolves into a real or more serious problem. After all, energy and life are not fixed but are always in a state of flux.

Healing Bad Energy

Sometimes people experience energy that causes them to be worried or anxious, making joy an elusive emotion. If you feel such negative energy settling over you, for whatever reason, you can do this exercise to restore healing and balance: First, close your eyes and take a few slow, relaxing breaths in through your nose and out through your mouth. Next, focus your full attention on the center of your heart and surround yourself with a golden light. Then, acknowledge three things that you love about yourself. As you acknowledge your lovable qualities, feel this flow of self-love and acceptance moving throughout your entire energy field. Next, if you know the source of your bad vibes, imagine it, too, being surrounded by white light. If you don't know the source, ask Divine Spirit to surround the unknown problem and remove it from your energy field. See yourself completely engulfed in love, appreciating, healing, calming, and balancing your vibration. Do this for two or three minutes. When you are finished, open your eyes.

Seven Ways to

GIVE YOURSELF JOY

1. When you wake up in the morning, give yourself three loving compliments.

2. Before you go to sleep, think of three good things that happened to you that day.

3. When you brush your teeth in the morning, look into your eyes and say, "I love you," and mean it.

4. During the day, pay attention to any subtle energy shifts, and ask your heart for guidance when anything is off balance.

5. Put a white loving light of protection around yourself every day.

6. Every three hours think of at least one thing that makes you laugh.

7. Appreciate yourself for making at least one creative choice a day.

Being aware of your intuition is only part of the process when it comes to living a centered and joy-filled life. Putting your intuitive guidance into action in the world is the other part. When you do that, you put a value on your intuition, and it can then begin to help you in life.

Trust your intuition and act
on its counsel.
Take a leap of faith into
the world of the extraordinary!

LOOK AT
THE STARS!

Noticing your intuition is like noticing stars. For the longest time you can go along never really seeing the night sky overhead. Then one night you look up and see sparkling stars in the sky. Taken by their lovely twinkle, you are drawn into the blackness, seeking more bright sky lights. At first you may see only a few, then more, then still more, until quite spontaneously your whole perception shifts and suddenly the skies seem to explode with thousands upon thousands of stars. It's humbling to realize that although these lights were in the sky all along, you are just noticing them for the first time.

Housecleaning

Here is a great tool for clearing old or stagnant
energy and bringing in fresh, joyful energy.
First, go outside, or,
if the weather is inclement, go into a quiet room.
Stamp your feet or, better yet, jump up and down
a few times and draw in a deep, cleansing breath.
Next, rub your hands over your aura
as though you were washing a windshield
and then shake them vigorously in the air.
Imagine yourself bathed in a loving white light
pouring in at the top of your head
and settling into your heart.
Imagine everything and everyone that
bothers you draining into the ground and away
from your aura. Now imagine a golden light
taking its place, filling your heart with joy and
spreading a warm glow throughout your body.

We need to pay very close attention
to how others' energy affects us
so that we can take steps to prevent it
from affecting us negatively.

establishing boundaries

One of the most important things you need to learn for a joyful life is to set boundaries so that others will not manipulate or invade you. Being aware of how other people's energy affects you is one important way to do this. This is intuitive self-defense, and using it gives you tools to identify trouble anywhere, anytime, and to move away from its source. Two of your best self-care tools are your feet. When you are exposed to any kind of soul-distressing energy, use them to leave. Get away from negativity as fast as you can; if necessary, even make up an excuse, such as "I don't know why, but suddenly I don't feel well. I need some fresh air." Don't just stand in the midst of negative energy and take it in. It will make you sick!

Here are some other great grounding techniques.

Take a brisk walk.

Garden.

Do the dishes.

Drum.

Dance or jump rope.

*Cook, bake bread, chop vegetables,
do the laundry.*

Give yourself a foot massage.

Go barefoot in the grass.

Down the Drain

If you are routinely bogged down
with negative energy, try this technique
to clear your spirit.

Imagine all the debris floating
in your aura.

Next, take in a long deep breath and
imagine this psychic debris leaving your aura
with your exhalation.

Inhale once again, filling your aura
with a cleansing golden light.

Repeat this two or three times.

Then carry on with your day.

Get Grounded

Cleanse negative energy and replace it with joy through a technique called grounding. Grounding means literally connecting your awareness to the ground. Running, jumping, exercising, touching the dirt, hugging trees, smelling flowers—all these activities will ground joy in your body and pull out unwanted negativity.

Walk it off.
Nothing restores you to your natural
state of inner joy more effectively
than a walk in nature. This is so
effective that you may want to
incorporate a short walk into your daily
routine just as an insurance policy for
health and happiness. Even twice
around the block will be sufficient to
drain away interference, eliminate
psychic pollution, and restore clarity
in your aura's field.

Everything that comes from your spirit,
however insignificant it may
appear or feel, counts.

Be Flexible

The function of intuition is to help guide you toward joy, toward making the best possible decisions in your life. Intuition serves to direct your attention to the best ways of achieving goals; it alerts you to potential problems and acts to keep you safely on your path. Therefore, it makes perfect sense that an intuitive feeling may very likely call for a change of direction or ask you to rethink your ideas on things. So be open. Be flexible. Be ready to follow your guidance at any given moment.

Be patient and trust your intuition, especially when it appears to inconvenience you or upset your plans. Keep an open mind, and respond with humor and flexibility. It's okay to be nervous at times, as long as you don't ignore what you are feeling.

remember:

Act on your intuition.

Be flexible.

Change your plans if necessary.

Speak up if you must.

Breathe into your fear.

Trust.

Laugh.

The most direct way to access
your intuition and find joy is to use
your imagination. Imagination is the
front door to your intuition.
Imagination creates the world!
It is not only the source of your intuitive
ability but also the source
of *all* your ability.

WONDER

An exciting way to activate your intuitive imagination is through wonder. Wonder sets the tone for your spirit to guide you to joy. It gets you out of your head and takes you into your creative and playful heart. It invites you to explore the unseen world with enthusiasm and open-mindedness. It helps you access the unknown, the spiritual and intuitive side of life and of yourself. Wonder directs your attention to options that you might have otherwise overlooked, and it keeps your awareness fresh and keen. And the best part is that it's fun.

Try this!

wonder:

who is calling when the phone rings

where you'll find a parking space

when the elevator will come

who people really are

how best to do your work

what your real talents are

what your heart desires

We need to laugh at our mistakes before we can learn from them. Laughter brings distance, perception, and sometimes insight. It also reminds us that who we are (spiritual beings, time travelers here on earth to create) and what we do (make mistakes) are not the same thing. Laughter keeps our self-worth intact even as it emphasizes the need to look foolish at times to gain discovery.

My mother always said,
"Remember to laugh.
The situation may be critical . . .
but it is never serious."

What is the most critical situation
you face right now?
What is humorous about it?

One of the easiest ways to ask the
Universe to support you is to close
your eyes, think of your problem or
challenge, and then say . . .

"help!"

The Universe put you here to have an adventure . . . and will provide all you need to have the best adventure! Keep your sense of adventure and allow the Universe to entertain you. Let adventure take you to:

A hike in nature

A foreign city

An ethnic restaurant

A jazz club

An experimental theater

A religious festival

A drumming circle

An improv class

The Universe is ready, willing, and able to guide you to joy just for the asking. But before Divine Spirit can assist you, you need to *ask* the Universe for help and guidance. Love, protection, safety, inspiration, solutions, and everything else you need to grow and thrive in life are available. When you are ready for support, the Universe is willing to support you.

Believe it or not, it's easy to be guided.
Simply tell the Universe what
you want . . . but don't tell it how.
Be open to surprise!

The most direct way to ask for help
is to pray. And one of the most powerful ways
to pray is to be thankful for what you have
right now. Gratitude affects our consciousness
like wipers affect a windshield
in a storm. It clears away confusion
and helps us see the world more clearly.
Practicing gratitude as a form of prayer is very
easy and is immediately rewarding.
All you need to do is to acknowledge and
thank the Universe for all your blessings:
good health, family, friends,
or simply being alive.

Practicing Gratitude

Being grateful instantly lightens the heart and helps us remember how much we are loved and supported by the Universe. Whenever you are feeling restless, irritable, anxious, bored, uneasy, or fearful, think of as many things as possible to be grateful for. List your blessings one at a time, trying to name at least ten things. Practicing gratitude keeps us focused on the abundance, support, and love that the Universe has for us. It focuses our hearts on receiving all that is available to us and reminds us to remain in a state of receptivity and peace.

How you pray for joy is very personal, and any prayer is valid. Pray in whatever way you want to, and use whatever approach or tradition feels right to you. Know that the Universe loves you completely and unconditionally as you are, faults and all. Whether praying alone or with others, realize that the Universe *wants* to help, would *love* to help. But first you must ask.

when in doubt:

Close your eyes,
put your hand on your heart,
and breathe.

Then ask Divine Grace to guide you.

Following your intuition is like
dancing with God.
As you move toward your soul,
your soul and the
Universe will move toward you!

Are you:

Being playful, having adventures?

Practicing gratitude?

Remembering to ask for help?

Aware that the Universe loves you
and wants to help?

Listening to your heart and following your intuition will instill in you a profound sense of confidence and security. It isn't a confidence that arises from an egotistical sense of "I can do it." Rather, it is a sense of relief, knowing that I don't have to do it on my own. I only have to do my part, and the Universe will meet me halfway with support, protection, and guidance.

The best part about listening to your
intuitive heart is that you'll see more
deeply into yourself and others.
Guess what?
You'll like what you see.

SPIRIT GUIDES

The Universe provides us with a group of spirit guides whose sole purpose is to assist, support, direct, protect, instruct, and delight us as we work to fulfill our purpose in life. We all have different spirit guides for different purposes. They help us in our day-to-day lives as well as with our physical, emotional, and spiritual development. Their only purpose is to make our lives easier, more enjoyable, and full of wonder. There are different types of guides, with their own intentions, and we all have these marvelous beings assigned specifically to us.

Your guides love you.
Your guides are there specifically
to help you. And when they help you,
they in turn are evolving ever upward
into the light of Divine Oneness.

With your guides' help, life will become even more joyful.

Your days will turn into adventures.

Loneliness and isolation will disappear.

You'll be surrounded by love.

You'll attract your heart's desire.

Life will be full of synchronicities.

Miracles will happen every day.

☆ Joy Guides

Especially fun are your joy guides. Joy guides are childlike essences whose purpose is to make you laugh. They invite you to play and to express yourself without self-consciousness. They twinkle past you all the time, trying to engage the child in you. They lighten you up, free your spirit, and amuse you.

Joy guides show up at the darnedest times. When pain seems too great to bear, they break the vibration, release the tension, and remind us that there is no death. They are funny, silly, irreverent, tricky, and sly. They like to shake up the drama and bring in the joy. A joy guide is always present at funerals to usher out the pain. They show up at somber moments and make you burst out laughing. Joy guides are here to remind you to enjoy the walk.

Things to Ask Your Joy Guides

Make me laugh when . . .

I'm feeling depressed.

I'm feeling grief.

I'm feeling afraid.

I'm feeling rejected.

I'm feeling blocked.

I'm feeling drained.

I'm feeling overwhelmed.

I'm feeling I'm missing the point.

I'm causing trouble.

I need to be stopped.

I need some air.

Help me recover and express my . . .

Creativity.

Playfulness.

Humor.

Silliness.

joy!

Get to Know
Your Guides

Your guides lovingly seek to serve you. Talk to
your guides. Give your guides names, or ask them
what their names are. You will be surprised with
what they tell you. Don't be shy. Ask your guides
to help you in every way that you need help.
Remember that they *want* to help.

One thing you will discover
when you begin to nurture intuition
is that you are nurturing your most
authentic self, your spirit.
Nurturing intuition is actually the art
of discovering and honoring
who you really are.

FOLLOWING YOUR HEART

Following your heart introduces you to a world that is friendly, adventurous, and joyful, but most of all one that welcomes your unique essence. It invites you to experience real joy in your life, the joy that comes from within, that cannot be diminished by anyone.

As you become more aware of your Higher Self and your soul, you'll make a very important discovery: even if your mind doesn't know it, your soul has never been lost. It knows exactly where it's going. If you allow yourself to be guided, you'll move directly toward your purpose in life with grace and ease. You'll also discover that it isn't very far away from where you are right now. You simply couldn't see it.

When you listen to your heart,
life becomes a joyous adventure.
Be open. Breathe. Meditate. Dance.
Wonder. Ask for help. Listen.
Trust. Explore. Leap into the world
of the extraordinary.

savor the magic!